SALAMUN 3ALA ISSA IBN MARYAM
سلام على عيسى ابن مريم
3:45 / 61:14

JOCKEY YOUNG'UNS

THE LEGEND OF KENTUCKY DERBY'S YOUNGEST WINNERS

BY BEST SELLING AUTHOR
SULTAN ZESHAN

ILLUSTRATED BY
DR. LORIN CHASAR

On a fine day in May of 1875, a sea of ladies and gentlemen in fine clothes and fancy hats watched as horses and jockeys thundered past on the brand-new Churchill Downs racetrack. Hearts pounded in time with hoof beats as everyone wondered who might pull ahead as the final stretch approached. In the blink of an eye, a chestnut horse named Aristides crossed the finish line first.

On his back was a jockey named Oliver Lewis, the very first winner of the Kentucky Derby.

A Black equestrian.

In the path he had blazed across that dirt track, who would follow?

Many miles away in Mossy Point, Mississippi, Alonzo Clayton did not have time to daydream about cheering crowds and glorious victories. He had eight brothers and sisters running around shouting, "Lonnnnnnieeeee!!" for him at all hours of the day to keep him busy.

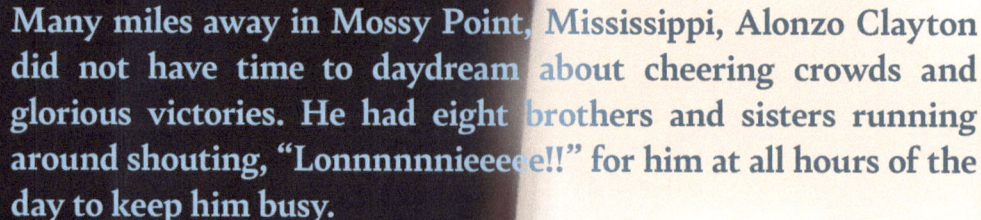

With such a big family, Lonnie had to help earn money, even at the age of ten. He went to school when he could, because he was a clever boy who liked to learn. But Lonnie was smart when it came to the business of making money too.

There was a guest at the local hotel who needed an errand run.

He was ready to take care of it!

Did a gentleman have scuffed shoes that needed polishing?

Soon, Lonnie would have them so shiny, he could see his reflection in them!

When he was twelve, Lonnie left behind his crowded home and odd jobs to start a career that would change his life forever. He joined his brother at Lucky Baldwin's Stud Farm in Chicago, Illinois. He would become a stable hand, helping to take care of the horses that were bred and trained there.

Lonnie's brother taught him something new: how to be an exercise rider for the horses on the farm. Every day, Lonnie rode the racehorses around the property to stretch their legs and strengthen their lungs. He was learning to ride, and the horses were learning to race. The men who worked at the farm watched Lonnie. He was a fast learner. A strong rider. A small and light boy. Maybe, they thought, he could be more than an exercise rider.

When they offered to train Lonnie as a jockey, he was eager to learn and to do his very best job. A jockey earned more than an exercise rider! Think of all the money he could send his family! At just fourteen years old, he put his heart and his focus into training, seizing the opportunity he had been given.

A year later, breathless and filled with pride, he crossed the finish line of the important Jerome Stakes race in first place. He was a real jockey—shining shoes was a thing of the past.

Soon, Lonnie was streaking down the track again, on the back of a bay horse named Azra. Together, they won the Champagne Stakes. They made a good team, thought Azra's trainer, John H. Morris.

And so, it was decided that Lonnie would train to ride Azra in the biggest race the horse and jockey had ever faced: the now-famous Kentucky Derby.

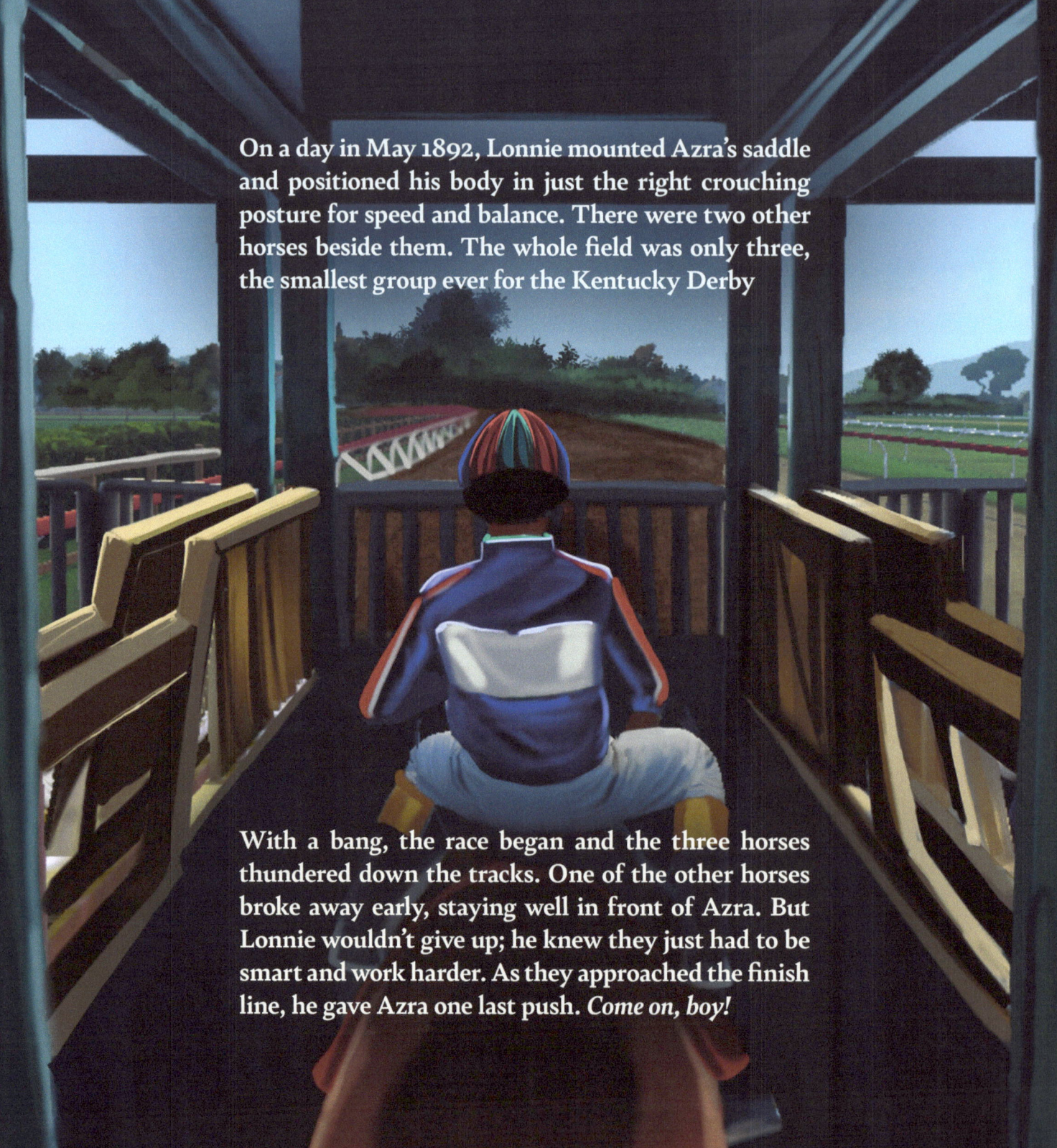

On a day in May 1892, Lonnie mounted Azra's saddle and positioned his body in just the right crouching posture for speed and balance. There were two other horses beside them. The whole field was only three, the smallest group ever for the Kentucky Derby

With a bang, the race began and the three horses thundered down the tracks. One of the other horses broke away early, staying well in front of Azra. But Lonnie wouldn't give up; he knew they just had to be smart and work harder. As they approached the finish line, he gave Azra one last push. *Come on, boy!*

Lonnie could see the wire across the finish line when they made their move, pushing as hard as they could for the lead. Two horses crossed the finish line together. But who was first?

Azra, by a nose! At just fifteen years old, Lonnie had become the youngest jockey to ever win the Kentucky Derby.

Nearby in Kentucky, a boy named James Perkins was growing up in a large, close-knit family with four siblings. His parents were previously enslaved people and wanted their children to have every opportunity and happiness they'd never had.

James's father was a horse trainer and he taught his sons everything he knew about raising and caring for horses. By the time James was nine, he was already at work in the stables, following in his father's footsteps.

James was small and young but he wouldn't let that stop him. At just eleven, he started entering races as a jockey, flying down the track on horses so big most children his age would be afraid to even mount them. With each race, he improved more and more, until a thirteen-year-old James shocked everyone by winning eleven races in a single day!

Anyone could see he was the perfect jockey: he was light as dandelion fluff, with an intuitive connection to horses and a fierce drive to win. So in 1892, James was offered a five-year jockey contract, which he accepted. The future, just as his parents had hoped, was bright.

James was dedicated to training for his career, no matter what he had to do. Soon he had a new nickname: Soup. James was a growing boy, but jockeys needed to stay lightweight, so he kept to a diet of mostly soup. Did James want to eat other delicious foods? Probably. But more than that, he wanted to be the best.

In 1893, brand-new jockey "Soup" Perkins made his debut on the racetracks. He won an unbelievable five races back-to-back. Soup's heart soared—on horseback, he was unstoppable!

In just that first year, Soup placed in 16 out of the 26 races he entered. The men he worked for watched in amazement as he improved day after day, bringing out the best in their horses. His parents watched with pride as he made his dreams come true—and theirs too.

They weren't the only ones watching, and not everyone was happy to see Soup succeed. In fact, many people were willing to do anything they could to stop Black jockeys from winning—or even competing—in horseracing.

Since the very beginning of the sport of horseracing in the United States, Black jockeys had been racing—and winning—for plantation owners. After the Civil War and Emancipation, these talented Black athletes had continued competing, but as employees, not slaves.

With horse racing becoming the largest and highest-earning sport in the country, there was a lot of money to be made for jockeys.

The Union of White Jockeys was formed with the goal of forcing Black jockeys off the track, so that white riders could have all of the prize money for themselves.

Soup Perkins wouldn't be intimidated. He had trained hard for the biggest race of his career—the Kentucky Derby—and he was focused and ready.

On a day in May 1895, Soup mounted Halma: a black stallion bred in Kentucky for hometown fans to cheer on. And there were lots of fans! Twenty-thousand people crowded the stands—the most of any Kentucky Derby ever.

With a pounding of hooves, the race began. Soup and Halma pulled right out in front of the crowd. But had they rushed ahead too early? Would Halma get tired and lose his lead? No! Soup and Halma flew down the racetrack together and won by five lengths.

In the Winner's Circle, reporters pushed and shoved to the front to ask Soup questions. How old are you? they wanted to know. Soup beamed with pride and answered, "Going on sixteen." At just fifteen years old, he had tied with Lonnie Clayton for youngest Derby winner ever.

Lonnie Clayton's wealth and fame were growing, race by race, win by win. Since the Kentucky Derby, he had taken home the prize at many other important races, like the Travers Stakes in New York and the Clark Stakes in Kentucky. He even rode Halma to his very first victory, before Soup Perkins rode him in the Kentucky Derby.

All of these wins meant Lonnie was earning enough money to make his dreams come true. Instead of spending his earnings, he invested them in a large, grand house for himself in Little Rock, Arkansas. The building style of the house is known as Queen Anne Victorian design. He also bought other buildings that would bring in more earnings. Lonnie had always been smart in the business of making money, ever since his days working odd jobs as a child. Now, his wealth from being a successful jockey would help him be a successful businessman

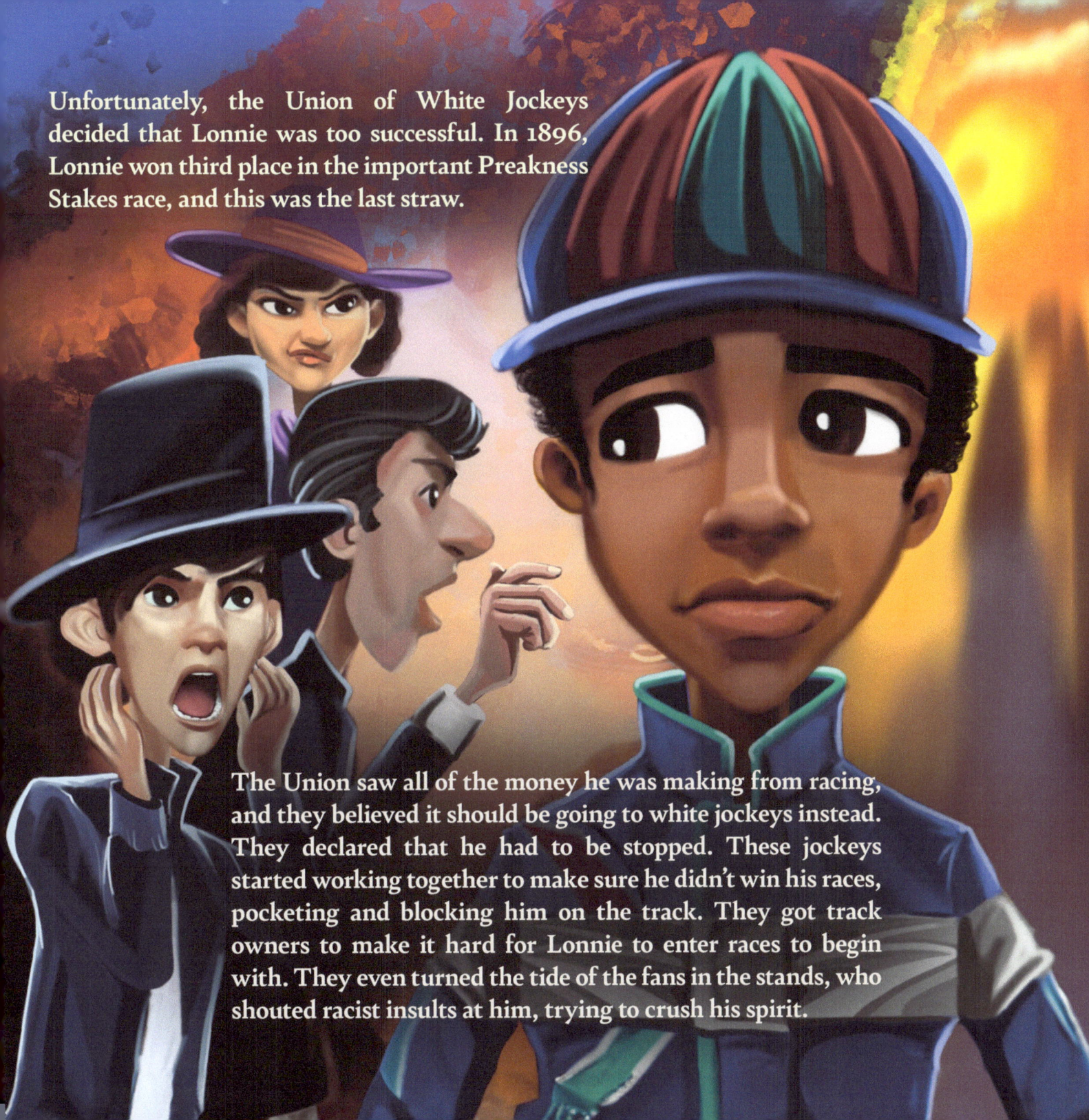

Unfortunately, the Union of White Jockeys decided that Lonnie was too successful. In 1896, Lonnie won third place in the important Preakness Stakes race, and this was the last straw.

The Union saw all of the money he was making from racing, and they believed it should be going to white jockeys instead. They declared that he had to be stopped. These jockeys started working together to make sure he didn't win his races, pocketing and blocking him on the track. They got track owners to make it hard for Lonnie to enter races to begin with. They even turned the tide of the fans in the stands, who shouted racist insults at him, trying to crush his spirit.

After he won the Kentucky Derby, James "Soup" Perkins' star was on an unstoppable rise. That same year, he won 192 more races, each with fame and prize money attached. Turfmen, racing fans, and reporters all had their eyes on his successful career, which was just beginning.

The Union of White jockeys had their eyes on his career too, and they wanted to put an end to it. In 1897, Soup was disqualified from a race by officials and suspended from the sport of horseracing. He would not be allowed to be a jockey anymore.

Soup was only twenty years old, and his incredible career as a jockey was over. What would he do after this crushing loss?

He was still determined to have a better future, just as his parents had always wanted for him. So he moved back to Lexington, Kentucky, got married, and made a new career buying and training horses. If there was one thing Soup Perkins knew how to do, it was to work with horses.

Lonnie had used all of his strength and determination to continue competing, in spite of the other jockeys' racism against him. He had struggled to be allowed to race and be treated with respect and decency. But the Union of White Jockeys has connections throughout the business, and they had plans to get Lonnie out.

At an important race in 1901, Lonnie was accused of cheating by fixing who the winner would be. After that, rumors flew. Turfmen and racetrack owners talked. It became very hard for Lonnie to enter races.

For Soup Perkins, there was more opportunity outside of the United States. In Canada, racism in horse racing was less fierce. He and his family moved to a new country, where he was able to start training horses to race without so many obstacles.

Lonnie's career as a jockey never recovered from the made-up scandal. So he was forced to retire in 1904. What would he do now?

Lonnie had always been resourceful. He moved to California, where he got a job working in a hotel, just as he had many years before.

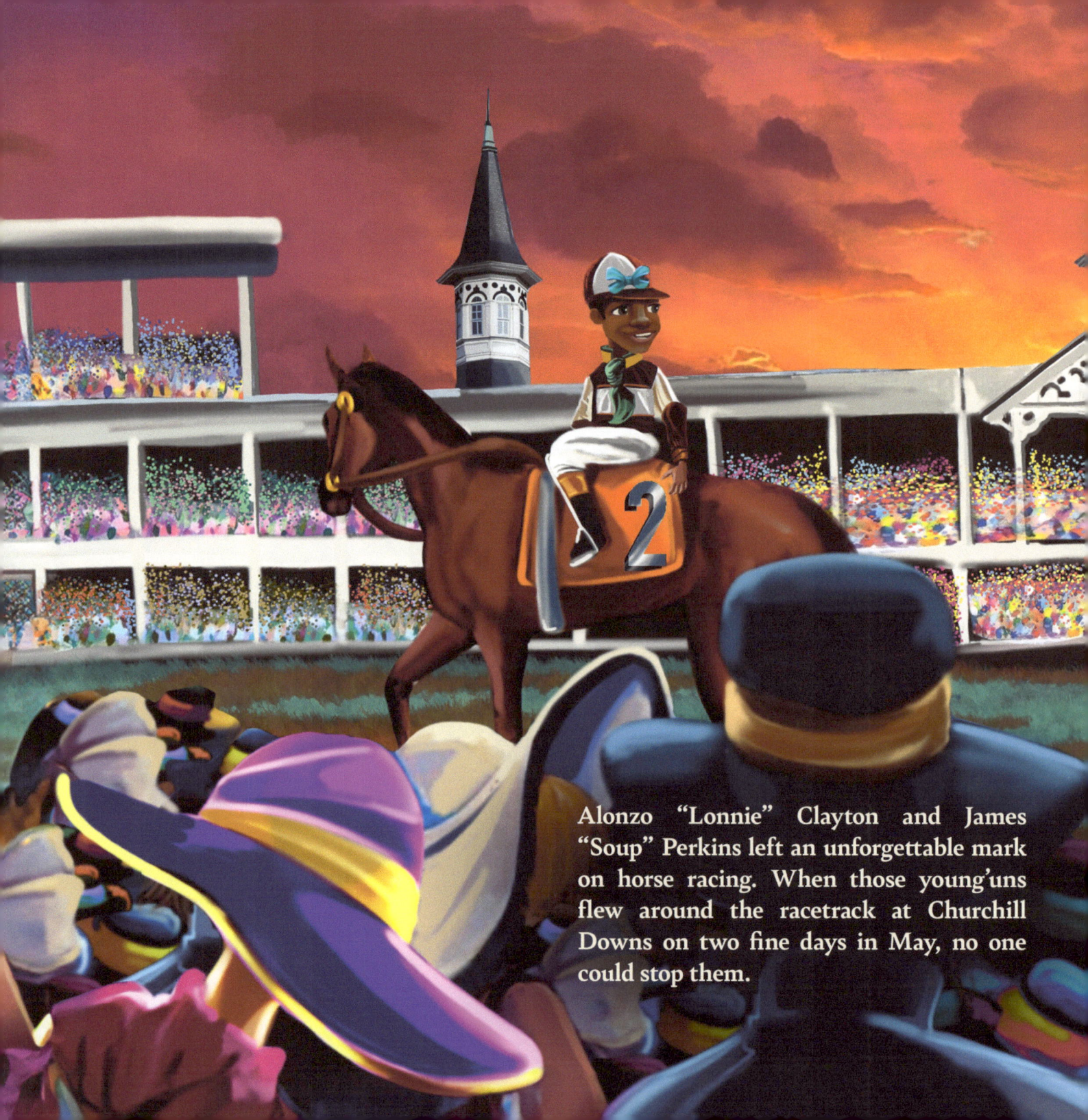

Alonzo "Lonnie" Clayton and James "Soup" Perkins left an unforgettable mark on horse racing. When those young'uns flew around the racetrack at Churchill Downs on two fine days in May, no one could stop them.

Their victories weren't just personal triumphs, but symbols of hope for all young dreamers. They proved that talent and determination know no color. Today, their spirit continues to inspire young'uns everywhere, reminding them that anyone can overcome adversity and achieve their dreams through hard work and determination. So dare to dream, like Soup and Lonnie!

TIMELINE

1875
The first Kentucky Derby is held at the newly-built Churchill Downs racetrack. It is won by a Black jockey named Oliver Lewis

1876
Alonzo "Lonnie" Clayton is born in Mossy Point, Mississippi

1879
James "Soup" Perkins is born in Lexington, Kentucky

1888
Lonnie Clayton begins working as a stable hand at Lucky Baldwin's Stud Farm in Chicago, Illinois

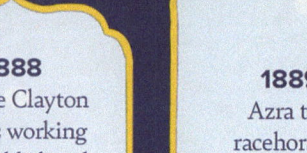

1889
Azra the racehorse is born

1895
Lonnie Clayton buys a Queen Victorian style home in North Little Rock, Arkansas

1895
"Soup" Perkins wins the Kentucky Derby at the age of fifteen, by five lengths, riding Halma

1896
Lonnie Clayton finishes third at the Preakness Stakes in Coney Island, New York

1897
"Soup" Perkins is disqualified from a race by officials and is suspended from horseracing indefinitely

1899
Having been forced out of horseracing, "Soup" Perkins moves to Lexington, Kentucky, where he marries and becomes a horse owner and trainer

TIMELINE

1890
Lonnie Clayton begins his professional horseracing career as a jockey

1891
Lonnie Clayton wins the Champagne Stakes riding Azra

1892
Lonnie Clayton wins the Kentucky Derby at the age of fifteen, riding Azra. He and Azra win the Travers Stakes this same year.

1892
"Soup" Perkins signs a five-year jockey contract and trains for competition. Halma the racehorse is born

1893
"Soup" Perkins makes his racing debut, placing in 16 out of 26 races

1904
Lonnie Clayton retires from working in horseracing after being forced out

1911
"Soup" Perkins dies of a heart attack in Ontario, Canada at the age of 32

1917
Lonnie Clayton dies of tuberculosis at the age of 40

2011
Part of a road in "Soup" Perkins' hometown of Lexington, Kentucky is renamed "Soup Perkins Alley" in his honor.

2012
Alonzo Lonnie Clayton is inducted in Arkansas Sports Hall of Fame

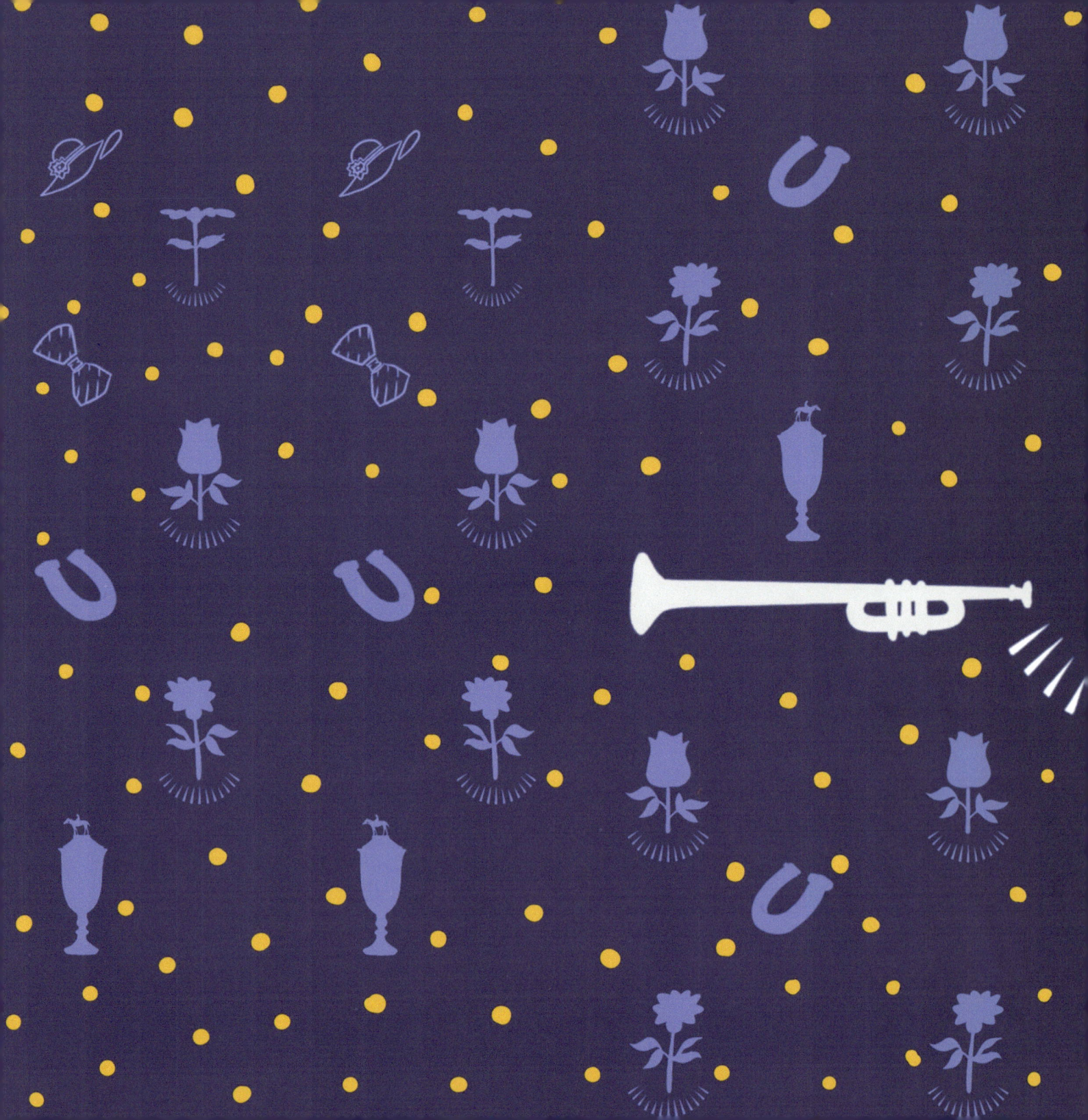

GLOSSARY

Jockey: A person whose job is to ride horses in races.

Derby: An annual race reserved for three-year-old horses.

Equestrian: A person who rides horses. Can also be used to describe anything that relates to horseback riding.

Stud Farm: A farm where race horses are bred and trained.

Exercise Rider: An equestrian who takes race horses out for their workouts to build strength and speed, preparing them for races. This is different than a jockey; exercise riders do not participate in races.

Stakes: A race in which part of the prize money is offered by the owners of the horses who enter. Their money is in the pot for the winner, so they have a "stake" in the result of the race.

Bay Horse: A term describing the color of a horse's fur. In this case, a horse with reddish-brown fur, who also has a black mane, tail, ear tips, and lower legs.

Wire: In a horse race, a piece of wire is stretched between two poles at the finish line. Whichever horse finishes the race first will be the one to tear the wire down. This is where the expression "down to the wire" comes from—it means that the outcome of something is not decided until the very last second, like a close horse race.

"By a Nose": In a horse race, if a horse is said to have won "by a nose," it means the victory was very narrow. The winner was only in front of the second place horse by the tip of his nose! This is why the wire is needed; whichever nose hits the wire first is the winner.

GLOSSARY

Civil War: A war in which a country breaks apart and fights against itself. In the United States, the North, known as the Union, fought against the South, known as the Confederacy, from 1861-1865.

Emancipation: The freeing of people who were previously enslaved. This happened in the United States through multiple actions. First, an executive order made by Abraham Lincoln on January 1, 1863 that said all enslaved people in the Confederate states were officially free under the law. The problem was, the Confederacy did not consider themselves part of the United States anymore, nor did they consider Abraham Lincoln to be their president. So enslaved people could only gain this freedom if they escaped their enslavers and fled to the Union states or were freed by the Union army. Secondly, after the Civil War ended, the thirteenth amendment to the U.S. Constitution was passed. This amendment, ratified in 1865, outlawed slavery or involuntary servitude throughout the United States, except as punishment for a crime.

Union of White Jockeys: An association of white jockeys that formed in the post-Civil War era with the goal of forcing Black jockeys off the tracks.

Stallion: A male horse.

Length: A measure of the distance between horses in a race, often used to describe how far the second-place horse was behind the winner. It counts the number of horses that could fit between the two contestants. One "length" is typically 8-9 feet, depending on the size of the horse being used to measure.

Turfman: A person who owns or trains racehorses and is passionate about the sport.

Commercial Property: A building that makes money for the owner through rent. Examples include a building that would be used for offices, a store, or a restaurant. Whoever is using the building for their business pays the person who owns it for the space.

AUTHOR'S NOTE

My time at Louisiana State University ignited a passion for Philosophy and African American history. Inspired by Dr. Stephen Finley and Dr. Martin, I discovered the often overlooked role of African Americans in horse racing. "Jockey Young'Un's" aims to rectify this, by sharing the untold stories of these trailblazers. Their important contributions to America's first sport, horse racing, have been unfairly overlooked for far too long. This book brings to light the inspiring stories of Alonzo Clayton and James Perkins, two African American jockeys. Despite facing challenges born out of their historical context, they reached remarkable heights in the horse racing world. The narrative begins with the foundation of the United States and its ideals of life, liberty, and happiness. Yet, these ideals were denied to many, including African Americans. Despite these barriers, Alonzo and James dared to chase their dreams. Born in the late 1800s, they emerged from families connected to the horse industry. Despite adversity, they broke records and made history in the prestigious Kentucky Derby. Unfortunately, both their careers ended early due to various challenges. This book includes a detailed timeline and biographies of Alonzo and James, offering more insight into their lives. I hope "Jockey Young'Un's" will inspire readers to appreciate the significant achievements of these two extraordinary individuals, and the wider, often overlooked contributions of African Americans to horse racing

*With affection and joy, this book is dedicated to our young'uns,
our beloved nieces and nephews,
by Sultan Zeshan & Lorin Chasar, Author & Illustrator.*

JOCTKEY YOUNG'UNS - The Legend of the Kentucky Derby's Youngest Winners
Text copyright © 2024 by Sultan Zeshan.

Illustrations by Dr. Lorin Chasar - Illustrations copyright © 2024 by Sultan Zeshan

Notice of Non-Liability and Fair-Use Disclaimer:
The information in this book is true and complete to the best of our knowledge. It is offered without guarantee on the part of the author. The authors, editors, and publishing vendors disclaim all liability related to the use of this book.

All rights reserved.

This book is protected under International and Pan-American Copyright Conventions. Reproduction, distribution, or transmission of the text and or illustrations, in whole or in part, in any form, whether electronic or mechanical, is strictly prohibited without the express written permission from Sultan Zeshan of Legendary Maestros LLC, except for brief quotations embodied in critical articles and reviews and certain other noncommercial uses permitted by copyright law.

Published in the United States by Project Equestrian X - Legendary Maestros LLC.

For permissions, contact: Email: projectequestrianx@gmail.com
Typography & Design: Safeer Ahmed copyright © 2024 by Sultan Zeshan
Editor: Sarah Jane Abbott

Library of Congress Control Number: 2023918173
IDENTIFIERS: LCCN (2023918173) (print) | LCCN (2023918173) (eBook)
| ISBN 978-1-959210-08-5 (hardcover) |
| ISBN 978-1-959210-09-2 (paperback) | ISBN 9781959210108 (eBook) |
| ASIN B0CRRQVMZ6 (Kindle) | Apple Books ID: 6475697654
Printed in the U.S.A. | FIRST EDITION

THE LEGEND OF KENTUCKY DERBY'S YOUNGEST WINNERS

JOCKEY YOUNG'UNS

BY BEST SELLING AUTHOR
SULTAN ZESHAN

ILLUSTRATED BY
DR. LORIN CHASAR

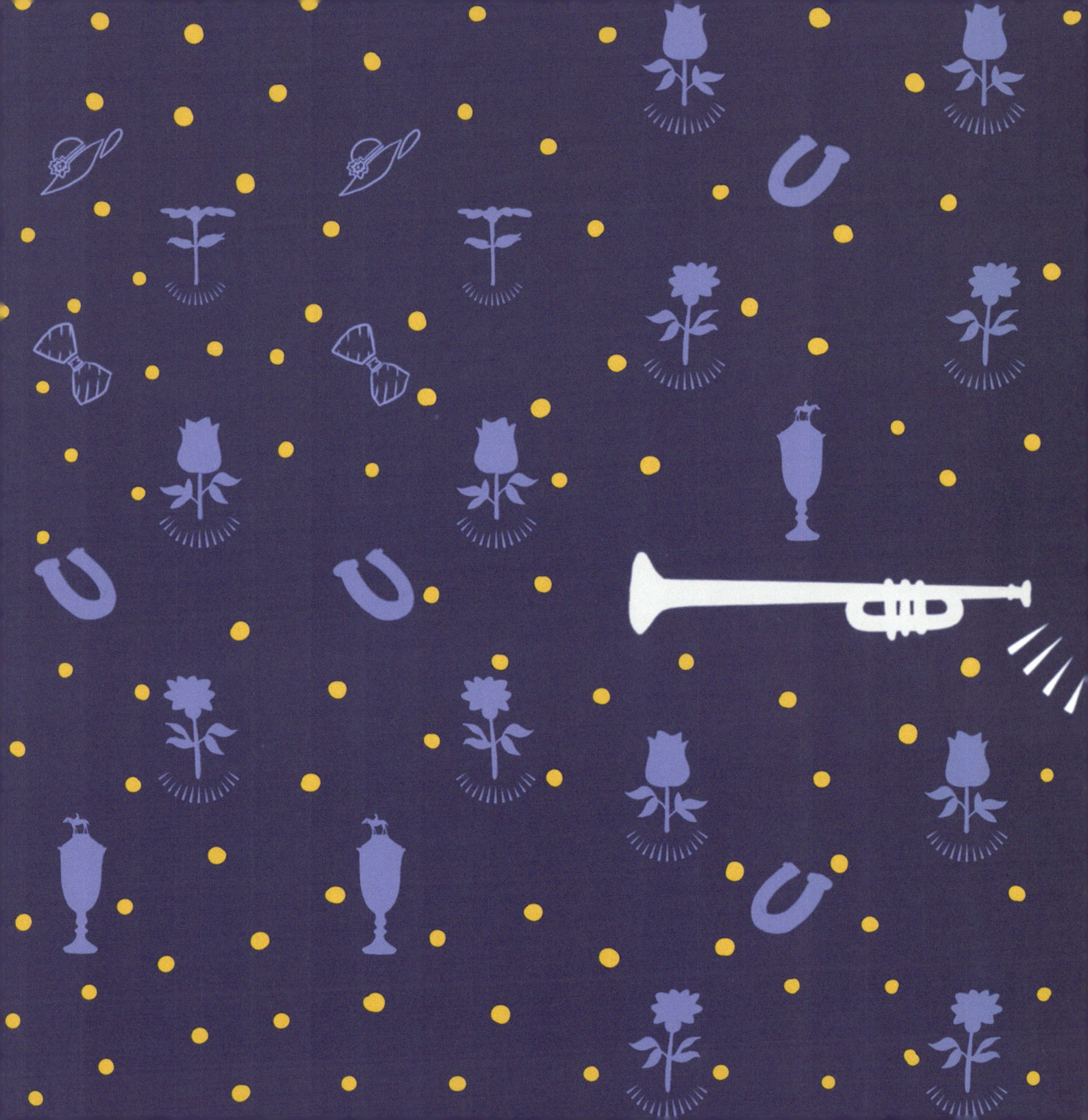

www.ingramcontent.com/pod-product-compliance
Lightning Source LLC
LaVergne TN
LVHW072114070426
835510LV00002B/48